READ THIS before buying Any Annuity!

by John L. Olsen, CLU, ChFC, AEP

Many statements about annuities are false or misleading. (Often, the author isn't lying; he simply doesn't know any better).

TRUE OR FALSE?   (Answers are at the top of the Table of Contents)

1. Annuities have high fees
2. Most annuity contracts don't impose ANY direct fees
3. Putting an annuity inside an IRA wastes the tax deferral
4. A "straight life" payout annuity offers a higher guaranteed income, per dollar invested, than ANY other instrument on the planet
5. If you have a "straight life" payout annuity and die "early", the insurance company keeps the rest of your premium
6. The average buyer of EVERY purely insurance product WILL NOT PROFIT from buying it.

Copyright John L. Olsen, 2017

All rights reserved. No part of this book may be reproduced in any form or by any electronic or mechanical means including information storage and retrieval systems – except in the case of brief quotations in articles or reviews – without the permission in writing from its publisher, John L. Olsen.

All brand names and product names used in this book are trademarks, registered trademarks, or trade names of their respective holders. I am not associated with any product or vendor in this book.

Published by Olsen Annuity Education.com

In Special Appreciation

This book is dedicated to the men and women of the United States Air Force, Army, Coast Guard, Marines, & Navy, past and present, who have shown us through their sacrifices just what the word "service" truly means.

Table Of Contents

True and False statements on Page One: Even numbered ones are true; Odd numbered ones are false.

READ THIS Before Buying Any Annuity! 1
Table Of Contents 4
Chapter 1 Introduction 5
   Why, and for whom, was this book written? 5
Chapter 2 Income, Starting Immediately 8
   I want an income, starting immediately (the Immediate Annuity) 8
      We're talking about Fixed Immediate Life Annuities 9
      PROS and CONS of Fixed Immediate Life Annuities 10
      What are Mortality Credits? 11
         Does it ever make sense to buy a "Life Only - No Refund" immediate annuity? 12
Chapter 3 Income, Starting At A Specific Time in the Future 14
   What if I want guaranteed income, but not until much later on? (The Deferred Income Annuity [DIA] or Longevity Annuity) .. 14
      An Investment vs. a Risk Management Tool 15
Chapter 4 - Accumulate Now, Take Income Later 17
   I want something that will grow my money over time (the Deferred Annuity) 17
   The Fixed Deferred Annuity 17
      The "Declared Rate" Fixed Deferred Annuity 18
   Surrender Charges? What Are Those? 19
      Why do surrender charges even exist? 19
      The Fixed Deferred Index Annuity ("Fixed Index Annuity") 23
      The Index went up 20% but my index annuity credited a lot less. Why? 24
   The Variable Deferred Annuity 28
Chapter 5 - Lifetime Income Riders 31
   The Guaranteed Minimum Income Benefit (GMIB) rider 31

    The Guaranteed Lifetime Withdrawal Benefit (GLWB) rider ...31
        The Central Promise: A Known Percentage of the "Benefit Base" 31
        The "Benefit Base" 32
Chapter 6 - Myths About Annuities 36
    "You can't lose money in an annuity" 36
    "Putting an annuity in an IRA 'wastes' the tax deferral of the annuity" 36
    "In an Index Annuity, the Insurer Keeps the Dividends on the Index Stocks" 38
    "Annuities Have High Fees" 38
    "Annuities Are Bad Investments" 38
    "I'm guaranteed at least a 6% return in that deferred annuity with a GLWB that has a 6% 'rollup' rate". 39
About The Author 40

Chapter 1 Introduction

Why, and for whom, was this book written?

This book was written for consumers (non-annuity professionals) who are considering the purchase of an annuity and who want to avoid making a mistake. This book is intended to be extremely *practical*. The focus is not upon the annuity contracts themselves but upon what an annuity of some sort can - or cannot - do for *you*.

Let me start by introducing myself. I am an annuity expert. My "bio" is printed at the end of this book. I've written or co-written four books on annuities and I consult, on a fee basis, with consumers and financial advisors who are trying to understand whether a particular annuity is in their best interest (or in the best interest of their clients). I'm not trying to sell you any annuity in this book (or in any other way, as I've retired from selling all insurance and investment products)

I am not in love with annuities and I don't hate them either. They're just **tool**s. Sometimes, a particular kind of annuity is the right tool for the job you want done; sometimes, it isn't. The way to find out whether it is or isn't is to *match the job to be done with the characteristics of the annuity contract you're considering*.

"Characteristics"? What's that mean? It means the things that that contract is designed to do and the ways in which it will try to do them. For example, some annuity contracts are designed to *accumulate* wealth over time. Others are designed to produce *income*, starting right away. Obviously, those are contradictory goals and an annuity that works well to achieve one of those goals won't work at all for the other one. To put it simply, there are many different kinds of annuity contracts and those different kinds are *very* different precisely because they are designed to do *very* different jobs.

In this book, I will try to explain, in plain English, what the various types of annuities are and how they work *so that you can make an informed decision as to whether buying some type of annuity is in your best interest.*

I've left out a great deal. There's nothing in here about the complicated *taxation* of annuities. If you're interested in that subject, I've written a book called "taxation and suitability of annuities for the professional advisor" that's available in paperback and as an e-book on my website - www.olsenannuityeducation.com. I've not dealt here with other extremely technical stuff, such as how insurance companies invest your premium when you've bought an annuity. My other books deal with those technical subjects in considerable detail. This book is for readers who want to know if the goals they have can be met by buying some kind of annuity.

DISCLOSURE: No book can give *all* the information possible on a given subject and this one doesn't try. Neither can any book be expected to give only totally accurate information with which no one could argue. Much of what's in this one is John Olsen's opinion. And I make no claims that everything in this book is 100% correct in all cases. I've written what I believe is true and tried to explain my reasons for the conclusions I've drawn and that's what you'll get.

I sincerely hope that this book will benefit you. If you have questions, you may email me at john@olsenannuityeducation.com, but I warn you that I will not be able to answer questions that are too complex - unless you wish to hire me for a fee. Short questions are fine, though. And, though I've said it already, I no longer sell products of any kind.

Warmest regards,

John L. Olsen, CLU®, ChFC®, AEP®
President: Olsen Annuity Education

Chapter 2 Income, Starting Immediately

Let's start by defining our terms. The word "annuity" simply means "a series of payments over time". It's an *income stream*. But most people don't use the word that way; for most of us, "annuity" refers to the *contract* that delivers that income stream (i.e.: "annuity contract"), and that's how we'll use the term here. Thus: "annuity" = "annuity contract".

Let's look at annuities in terms of what you, the potential buyer, want the annuity to do for you.

I want an income, starting immediately (the Immediate Annuity)

If you want an income to begin immediately (or within one year), you'll want an ***immediate annuity*** (also known as "payout annuity" or "income annuity"). There are two types:

1. A *Fixed Immediate Annuity*. This contract will *guarantee* an income that will last for a specified period of years (the "***period certain***" type) or for one or two lives ("***life annuity***"). The *amount* of each annuity payment will be *guaranteed*. It may be level over time or it can increase by a certain percentage (a "cost of living adjustment [COLA]) each year. At the end of the period, there will either be no value remaining or, if it's a life annuity and you've elected to include a "refund feature" and you die before receiving back all that you invested, the remainder will be paid to your beneficiary (I'm oversimplifying here, but that's basically how it works). With an immediate annuity, there is no *accumulation* or *cash value*. It's all about *income*.

2. A *Variable Immediate Annuity*. This works just like its fixed cousin except that the amount of each year's annuity payment will vary with the *investment performance* of the investment accounts (similar to

mutual funds) that you choose.

What do you mean by "Refund Feature"?

A life annuity will pay an income for the life of the annuitant. If he or she dies shortly after income payments begin, the contract will expire without value unless the buyer elected a "refund feature" - a guarantee that, in this situation, payments will continue to the beneficiary until all the money invested has been paid out. (That's the "cash refund" option, the most commonly chosen refund feature. There are other types, but they work in roughly the same way). Of course, if a refund feature is elected, the amount of the annuity income will be less than if there were no refund feature. (It's a trade-off). Not incidentally, in the "life only - no refund" annuity, the insurance company *does not "keep the rest of the money"*. It uses it to pay income to those annuitants who did not die early. That's how risk pooling works._My friend Jack Marrion pointed out to me that "refund feature" sounds like the buyer gets something back and that's not how it works of course. He suggested the term "return feature", which I confess sounds a lot more like what it actually does. But I'm going to stick with "refund feature" because that's the language insurance companies use in their policies and, often, in their marketing material.

We're talking about Fixed Immediate Life Annuities

Because very few consumers buy *"period certain"* immediate annuities (which pay for a specified period, whether the annuitant is alive or nor, and expire without value at the end of that period) or *variable* immediate annuities, we'll focus here on the immediate annuity that is popular and getting more so as our population ages - the **Fixed Immediate Life Annuity**.

What do you mean by "annuitant"?

The "annuitant" is the person whose age and sex determine the amount of each income payment. Usually, but not always, the annuitant is also the contract *owner* (the party who has all rights under the contract and to whom the annuity payments are taxable).

PROS and CONS of Fixed Immediate Life Annuities

The name says what it does. "*Fixed*" means that the amount of each annuity payment is fixed in advance. It will either remain level or increase by a specified percentage each year. "*Immediate*" means that income must commence within one year. "*Life*" means that the income will persist for the entire lifetime(s) of the annuitant or annuitants. (If there are two annuitants, the contract is called a "Joint and Survivor" annuity; no insurer offers this type to more than two annuitants).

Immediate life annuities are *all about income*. If you want the money in your contract to grow, or if you don't want your income to start for some years, they're not for you. However, if you want *guaranteed* income, starting immediately, for your entire remaining lifetime - this might be just the ticket.

What's so good about an immediate life annuity? What will it do that some other instrument won't?

If you buy any other instrument with the goal of providing yourself with an income for life, you've got only two choices. You can "live on the interest" produced by that instrument or you can take the interest and "tap" the *principal* periodically (if the amount of interest is insufficient). In the first case, you'll always have the value of the instrument to fall back on. In the second, you run two risks: First, the interest amount will decline over time (because there is less principal to earn interest), and, second, when the principal is exhausted, your income from this source will cease.

But with an immediate life annuity, *you cannot run out of money or suffer decreases in the amount of income.* That's the chief advantage of this beast: *The income will last as long as you do.* Moreover, the *amount* of each income payment may be greater than you can get from any other instrument.

I get more money from this thing than I could get elsewhere? How can that be?

You may get a higher return from some other investment, but that's rarely, if ever, possible on a *fully guaranteed basis*. And there's a reason for this - "mortality credits".

What are Mortality Credits?

Insurance companies know, with a very high degree of certainty, how many persons of a very large group of people of a given age will die each year. Some buyers will "die early". Some of those will have chosen the "life only - no refund" payout option (which offers the highest guaranteed income amount, but payments will cease upon the annuitant's death). Others will have chosen the "refund feature", which means that the insurer will have to pay out only the premium received. Still others will outlive "life expectancy". Because insurers know *how many* of the total of annuity buyers will fall into each group, they can use the money "left behind" by those who "died early" to increase the amount of the annuity payments that will eventually be received by the last group - those who live beyond life expectancy. That increase is called a "mortality credit", and only annuities offer it. The income produced by principal and interest alone will *never* be as great as that produced by principal, interest, and mortality credits. In fact, a "life only - no refund" immediate annuity *will always* produce a higher annual income, *on a fully guaranteed basis,* that can be obtained from any other instrument. And even one with a refund feature *may* produce more income than any available alternative.

"Period certain" annuities (those which persist for a given number of years, whether the annuitant is alive or not) **do not** offer mortality credits (which, when you think about it, just makes sense).

So what's the catch? What's not so good about immediate life annuities?

Of course, there's a trade-off. With that "life only - no refund" annuity, the contract will expire without value at your death, even if you die shortly after purchasing it. Most people don't like that, which is why most immediate life annuities are issued with a "refund feature", that guarantees that the insurer will pay out all of the premium received, either to the annuitant or the beneficiary. With that refund feature, the annuity income will be less than without it.

But in any case, an immediate annuity always involves *spending your principal*. The income is not just interest; it's interest, plus a return of some of the money you invested (your principal). Immediate life annuities are also fairly rigid. You usually cannot change your mind once payments have commenced or take more than the stipulated income (although some newer contracts do offer limited access to more than the stipulated income, with the understanding that subsequent income payments will be reduced as a result).

Moreover, you *should not* put money into one of these that you hope will pass to your heirs, because *no immediate annuity will guarantee a survivor benefit if you live long enough to get all your premium back*. If you do, you'll still receive that income for as long as you live, but the contract will expire without value when you die. (Again, I'm discussing the "cash refund" type of refund feature; there are other types in which the refund benefit depends upon how long the annuitant lives. But the principle is the same: If you live long enough, there will be no refund benefit!

Does it ever make sense to buy a "Life Only - No Refund" immediate annuity?

Very few people buy this type of annuity contract (sometimes called a "straight life annuity"), chiefly because they hate the idea that almost everything they contributed can be "lost" if they die shortly after buying it. (It's not "lost", but used to pay annuitants who haven't died, but, in the view of many prospective buyers, that still amounts to "lost money"). But for some people, in some situations, it can make a lot of sense. Let's start with the chief "defect" in this beast, as perceived by most people - the lack of any "legacy benefit", no matter what. Does that matter? If you have no one to whom you wish to leave money at your death, the lack of any death benefit shouldn't matter, particularly if that results in an income for you, for your entire lifetime, that is higher than you could possibly get on a fully guaranteed basis from any alternative.

But what if you have heirs? Again, this is a risk management problem, not an investment one. if the risk is not leaving enough to heirs and the "insured peril" is dying in that condition, then the most efficient solution is generally life insurance, which can produce more net, after-tax dollars to heirs per dollar spent to buy it than any other instrument. There is nothing to prevent you from purchasing, say, a life annuity with no refund to maximize your income for as long as you live and life insurance, to provide the legacy benefit the life only annuity does not. Indeed, this is a strategy commonly employed by sophisticated clients.

Chapter 3 Income, Starting At A Specific Time in the Future

What if I want guaranteed income, but not until much later on? (The Deferred Income Annuity [DIA] or Longevity Annuity)

A *"Deferred Income Annuity" (DIA),* also called a *"longevity annuity"* will guarantee you a specified income for life, starting at an advanced age (often, age 85). Many people fear that they may run out of money in late retirement (perhaps because they'll need more money each year than the portfolio earns and those "excess" withdrawals eventually exhausts the portfolio). There are two basic types: (1) the "pure" longevity annuity and (2) the deferred income annuity. *(These are my labels; some commentators use the first one, others use the second one, to describe either contract).*

The *"pure longevity annuity"* guarantees to pay you an income for life once you reach a specified age, but if you die before that age, the contract expires without value. (There's no "pre-Annuity Starting Date death benefit"). However, it may offer a refund feature once annuity payments commence.

The *"deferred income annuity"*, a newer form, offers the guaranteed income (and refund feature, if desired), plus a death benefit if you die before the Annuity Starting Date. It may also allow you to change that date after purchase. **Neither type offers a cash surrender value.**

Why would anyone want to buy something like that? I've heard many times that a longevity annuity, particularly the type that expires without value if you die before income is to begin, is a terrible investment. And I would agree. It would be a very terrible investment - if it were an investment. But it's not. It's a *risk management* tool.

An Investment vs. a Risk Management Tool

While they may often appear to be similar, there's a fundamental difference between an *investment* and a *risk management* (insurance) instrument.

Investments are all about <u>acquiring profit</u>.

Insurance is all about <u>avoiding loss</u>.

While many financial instruments have both investment and insurance features, it's very important to recognize the *main purpose* of the instrument you're considering. In my opinion, the Deferred Income Annuity - and, especially, the "pure" longevity version - is almost entirely a risk management tool. More specifically, it's a risk *transfer* tool. What's the risk? It's running out of income when you're too old to work to earn income. When you buy a DIA, you *transfer* that risk to the insurance company. It's no different from auto insurance, really. There, the risk (actuaries call this the "insured peril") is incurring expenses as a result of an auto accident and the risk is transferred from you, the buyer, to the issuing insurer.

But what about the fact that if I die early, all I invested is lost?

That's a fair question. If we were considering an *investment*, losing everything if you die early would make it a horrible investment. But we're considering a *risk transfer* tool - an insurance policy. The risk occurs if you're over 85 (or whatever the age to start income is) and you need income to live on. When you reach that age, the policy will pay the benefit because the insured peril occurred. But if you'd died before that age, the insured peril did not occur. (Dead people don't need income).

Yes, the premium never produced a benefit for you, but the same thing happens when you buy auto insurance and don't have an accident. Remember, this is *insurance*. Designed to avoid, offset, or minimize *loss,* not to provide a *profit.* In fact, **no pure insurance instrument will EVER be profitable to the average buyer.** If it were, the insurer would swiftly go broke. Ordinary, honest people don't buy insurance with the expectation of profiting thereby.

As for the objection to the "pure" longevity annuity that your heirs "lose everything you invested" if you die early, the answer is that providing a legacy benefit wasn't the purpose of the insurance. For that, life insurance is the obvious solution. NO single instrument will be ideal for meeting every financial need.

Chapter 4 - Accumulate Now, Take Income Later

I want something that will grow my money over time (the Deferred Annuity)

Here, neither an immediate annuity nor a deferred income/longevity annuity is appropriate, because neither has a cash value that will grow over time and that can be accessed when you need money. However, if the goal is to *accumulate* wealth, a deferred annuity might be a good bet. "Deferred" just refers to the fact that you can choose when your regular annuity income will commence. In newer contracts, you can defer receiving income practically forever. (Some contracts require that you begin taking income at some advanced age such as age 95). There are two basic deferred annuity types: (1) Fixed Deferred Annuity, and (2) Variable Deferred Annuity.

The Fixed Deferred Annuity

Again, the name tells us what this beast does. It's "fixed", which means that the units by which the annuity value is denominated are fixed; they don't vary over time. In the United States, those units are U.S. Dollars. By contrast, as we'll see, *variable* deferred annuities are denominated in either "accumulation units" (prior to annuitization) or "annuity units" (after annuitization), and those units change in value just about daily. "Deferred" means that the owner can defer the Annuity Starting Date (ASD), the point at which the contract will be "annuitized" (converted into an income stream under a chosen annuity payout option), almost indefinitely (or, at least, until some very advanced age). "Annuity" means that the contract can be used to create an *annuity* income (where payments will consist of both principal and interest).

The fixed deferred annuity, like its variable cousin, has two "phases" - the *accumulation* phase, prior to annuitization, and the *payout* (or *annuity*) phase, from annuitization until the contract expires (at the death of the annuitant or end of the "period certain"). During the accumulation phase the contract can earn interest. The manner in which interest is earned and credited depends upon whether it's a *declared rate* annuity or an *index* annuity.

The "Declared Rate" Fixed Deferred Annuity

This is the traditional kind of fixed deferred annuity and has been around for a long time. It offers several key benefits:

A guaranteed minimum rate of interest. While the contract may credit "current" interest at a rate which may change each crediting period, the minimum interest credited will never be less than a rate specified in the contract. Interest may be credited daily or less frequently.

Non-guaranteed "current" interest. Nearly all contracts of this type offer the possibility of interest earnings greater than the rate guaranteed in the contract. Typically, this "current" rate is declared at the beginning of each interest crediting period (which may be 1 year or several years).

Guaranteed annuity payout factors. If and when the owner elects to annuitize all or part of the contract, the amount of income for each payout arrangement (e.g.: "life and cash refund") will never be less than that calculated by the guaranteed payout factors in the contract.

A guarantee of principal. You'll always get back at least the amount you invested, *provided that you do not incur surrender charges.*

There are two types of "Declared Rate" Fixed Deferred Annuity: (1) The "Annually Declared" type and (2) the "Multi-Year Declared Rate" type.

The "Annually Declared" Fixed Deferred Annuity

In this type, current interest is declared annually, for the next year. It can never be less than the *guaranteed minimum rate* in the contract.

The "Multi-Year" Declared Rate Fixed Deferred Annuity

In this type, the interest crediting period is greater than one year. It may be from two to ten years. (There may be some contracts with crediting periods longer than ten years, but I've never seen one). Typically, the interest rate guarantee persists for the same number of years as the surrender charge period, so that, at the end of the period, a new interest rate is declared for the next period and the policy owner can surrender the contract without surrender charges (though there may be a tax penalty if he or she is under age 59 1/2).

Surrender Charges? What Are Those?

Surrender charges are probably the most controversial and misunderstood aspect of deferred annuities. A surrender charge is a percentage of any withdrawal from or total surrender of the annuity contract that will be forfeit to the insurance company if that withdrawal or surrender (a) exceeds a specified percentage of the account value **and** (b) is made during the *surrender charge period*. Darn! That sounds pretty harsh, and not very attractive. What's the reason for those charges? Why do surrender charges even exist and why should a potential buyer of an annuity put up with them?

Why do surrender charges even exist?

Surrender charges exist because insurers know that if the buyer surrenders the policy within the first few years after purchase, the insurer will lost money. This is because it costs that insurer money to ""put the business on the books". It incurs "acquisition costs", including sales commissions paid to the selling agent, underwriting and issue costs, ordinary costs of running the business, etc. Typically, the insurer recovers those costs from the excess of the interest it earns on invested premiums and the interest it credits to the policies. It takes *years* for full recovery to occur. There are basically four methods an insurer can use to offset the loss produced by some policy owners' surrendering their policies early.

A "front end sales charge"

The insurer could take a percentage of the premium received and not credit it to the annuity. In years past, this was commonly done, but it proved so unpopular that almost no commercial annuities are sold with front-end sales charges.

Crediting less interest than it otherwise would

The insurer could divert part of the interest it would normally credit to policies to a "loss recovery fund". This would, however, make the contract uncompetitive with contracts that credit more interest (because they impose surrender charges) and few consumers would purchase it.

Impose annual charges on all purchasers

The insurer could charge every buyer an annual charge to pay for the losses it experiences from early surrenders. This isn't likely to be popular, if for no other reason than that consumers don't like to pay charges. Besides, it's hardly fair.

Impose surrender charges on only those buyers who surrender the policy early

This method has the obvious advantage of being *fair*. The only people who pay charges designed to offset the insurer's loss for early surrenders are those who actually surrender early. Those who do not surrender early (or take more than the "penalty free withdrawal amount" in any year in the surrender charge period) will **never** pay for the losses that they did not cause to happen.

That said, there are annuities sold today that do not impose surrender charges. Those are almost always policies that do not pay a selling commission.

Can't I just buy an annuity that pays no commission and avoid surrender charges?

Yes, you can. Though there are fewer annuities out there of this type, they do exist. You can buy them directly from an insurer or from an advisor who is compensated by advisory fees.

In the first instance, you'll get only advice from a company representative, and this advice is typically limited. That is, it generally deals only with the annuity itself. You should not expect an insurance company's "customer service" representative to address your total financial picture; indeed, those people are generally *forbidden* by the insurer and state laws to do "financial planning". Nor should you expect an objective comparison of the insurer's own product with competing products. That said, if you're willing and able to do the research necessary to make a fully informed buying decision if you've "done your homework" and know what you want, this would be a good way to go.

If you're getting an annuity from a financial advisor whom you're paying for financial advice, you shouldn't be paying a commission. Some advisors do engage in "double dipping" (collecting both advisory fees and sales commissions) but that's generally considered unethical and is, in some states, illegal. In some states, advisors are permitted to charge advisory fees and credit sales commissions against those fees. That's an arrangement that I personally like a lot. However, it's illegal in some states.

Why would you need the advice of an agent?

That's a fair question. In my purely personal opinion, a sales commission that pays an agent only for selling a policy, where that agent is not committed to offering ongoing advice and monitoring of the performance of the annuity, is a bad deal for consumers. This is because many -indeed, most - annuity contracts cannot be placed on "autopilot". Client situations change. Goals and needs change. And the annuity contracts themselves often contain multiple options that must be considered in the light of changes in the client's needs and circumstances. The agent's commission *should* compensate that agent, not only for making the sale but also for providing ongoing counsel. Most professional agents are fine with this and many of us insist upon annual reviews with our clients.

Can't I "Do It Myself"?

Of course you can. It will take time and effort because the determination of what kind (if any) of annuity is appropriate for any particular consumer is not a simple process. Done right, it takes into account *all* of the consumer's needs and wants and financial situation. But it's not Rocket Science. If you're willing and able to do the work to ensure that you're making the right decision, you needn't pay someone else to do it. You'll need to research "no load" annuities, to see what's available in your state.

Some advisors work on a fee basis where they'll help you buy such an annuity, charging you only for the time he or she spends with you in putting the annuity in force. That arrangement, however, may be less available in the future, due to recent legislation such as the Department of Labor's "fiduciary duty" rule that may restrict advisors who do not commit to ongoing advice and monitoring.

The annuity I'm considering contains a "Market Value Adjustment". What is that?

A "market value adjustment" to the value of a deferred annuity when amounts are withdrawn **during the surrender charge period** is a mechanism to compensate the issuing insurer for the risk that the contract owner will withdraw money when the market value of the assets backing the annuity (bonds) is low. As interest rates and bond prices move inversely, this means that if interest rates rise after the contract is issued, bond prices will be lower; but it's when interest rates are rising that annuity owners typically want to surrender their existing contracts in order to purchase new contacts with more attractive interest crediting rates. (Typically, renewal rates on fixed annuities are less attractive in rising interest environments than the rates on new contracts).

But the MVA does not always reduce the surrender value of a deferred annuity because it is a *risk sharing* feature. If interest rates, years after the issue of a contract, have *declined*, bond prices will generally be higher; in that scenario, the MVA would be *positive* - that is, it would *increase* the surrender value of the annuity. I've seen cases where a positive MVA has actually increased the "net cash-in value" of a deferred annuity by more than the surrender charge. Typically, the MVA is calculated on only the amount withdrawn in excess of the "penalty free" withdrawal and expires at the end of the surrender charge period. The MVA is not always present in a deferred annuity contract, so you should *always* check to see if it's there in any contract you're considering buying.

Precisely how a given MVA operates varies from contract to contract. Often, there's an upper limit on how much it can increase or reduce the contract value, such as a percentage of contract value. In my opinion, in a very low interest environment such as we have now, the presence of an MVA is a cause for some concern, because a significant rise in interest rates could result in an MVA that might wipe out most, or even all, credited interest. That said, proponents of this feature argue that its inclusion allows the insurer to offer benefits more liberal than they could afford without this "risk sharing" feature.

The Fixed Deferred Index Annuity ("Fixed Index Annuity")

The other kind of fixed deferred annuity (in addition to the "Declared Rate" type) is the **Fixed Index Annuity** (often called simply the "Index Annuity"). Although a *fixed* annuity, like the "declared rate" type, it is *very* different in how it determines and credits interest.

The first thing to note about the index annuity is that interest is not credited *prospectively* (that is, for the coming period), but *retrospectively* (that is, for the interest crediting period that has just ended). The second thing is that interest in this type of annuity is *linked* to the positive performance of an external index, often (but not always) an *equity* index such as the S&P500®. Newer contracts usually offer a choice of indices, where the policyowner can elect one or more indices.

The Index went up 20% but my index annuity credited a lot less. Why?

The interest is credited, based on the positive movement of the index (the dollar value of the index, usually - but not always - without regard to dividends on the stocks in that index), adjusted by the application of one or more "moving parts" that have two major, and somewhat obvious, effects: (1) to reduce the insurer's risk (liability) and (2) to limit the amount of interest that will be credited. A third effect, not so obvious, is that they allow the insurer to offer index-linked interest in the first place. Without the risk-limiting moving parts, an insurer would probably choose not to enter the index annuity marketplace.

The "Moving Parts" in an Index Annuity

The usual moving parts are:

The **"Participation Rate"** - the percentage of positive growth in the external index that will be credited to the annuity; if the index rises by 20% and the participation rate is 60%, the annuity will be credited with 12% interest (assuming no other "moving part" is applicable).

The **"Interest Rate Spread"** - an alternative to the participation rate. Here, the insurance company retains the first N% of positive index growth and credits the remainder to the annuity contract. So, if the index rises by 20% and the interest rate spread is 5%, the annuity gets 15% interest.

The "**Cap Rate**" - is an upper limit on interest crediting. The *index rate cap* is the maximum percentage of positive index growth that will be recognized for interest crediting purposes. The *interest rate cap* is the maximum interest rate that will be credited. Most contracts today use the *interest rate cap* method.

Averaging. Many index annuities employ some form of averaging, in which it's not the value of the index at one point in time that is used in the interest crediting formula, but the average of that index value over a period, which may be monthly, annually, or over a period of several years. Averaging tends to smooth out interest crediting and protects the annuity owner from drastic end-of-crediting term losses that could otherwise wipe out a significant gain.

Interest Crediting Methods in Index Annuities

It is very important that we understand that in an index annuity, interest is credited *retrospectively* - that is, at the end of and interest crediting period (which may be one year or several years). The owner of an index annuity cannot know, *during* a credited period, how much interest will be credited to his or her contract at the end of that period.

There are many methods used today to credit interest in index annuities. Here are a few of the most common ones. A thorough discussion would take a lot more

The "Annual Point to Point" Method (AKA "Annual Reset")

The simplest, and most common, is the "Annual Point to Point" method. Here, at the end of each year the value of the index is compared with its value at the beginning of the period. If the index has risen in value, the percentage difference is determined and the "moving parts" are then applied to that difference to determine how much of it will be credited to the contract as interest. If the index has declined in value, zero percent interest will be credited. This is a common feature in index annuities - that *losses* in the index *will not* create losses in the annuity contract.

The "Monthly Sum" Method

This method is used when the interest crediting period is one year and calculates interest like this:
1. Calculate the index percentage change for each of the 12 months
2. Apply the monthly cap rate for each month with a positive change
3. Add the 12 results together. This is the interest rate to be credited.

The "Monthly Averaging with a "Cap" Method

Like the monthly sum method, this is used in contracts with an interest rate crediting period of one year. The calculation is done as follows:
1. Calculate the index percentage change for each of the 12 months
2. Add those 12 percentages
3. Divide by 12
4. Apply the contract's cap rate. The result is the interest rate to be credited.

The "Term End Point" Method

This is a method used where the interest crediting period is several years. The calculation works like this:
1. Determine the percentage gain over the period ([ending value - beginning value]/beginning value).
2. Apply the participation rate
3. The result is the total interest percentage to apply to the beginning value as interest.

There are many more methods than these few available today, but these are the most common. A recent innovation is volatility controlled contracts, in which the contract values are shifted between the indexed account(s) and a fixed account to reach a pre-determined volatility level. Typically, these contracts offer "no caps"; that is, the amount of interest is not limited by a "cap". However, "no caps" does not mean "unlimited upside performance", as the shifting to and from the conservative fixed account will ensure that the contract performance will never be as great as the best-performing index. A typical term end point index annuity only credits interest realized from index movements at the end of the term. For this reason, withdrawals from one of these contracts would forfeit any interest on the withdrawn funds that might have been credited had the money been retained in the contract until the end of the term.

"Managed Volatility Indices" methods

An index annuity crediting method that has become very popular in the past couple of years is the "managed volatility" strategy. As its name indicates, it seeks, not merely the most growth possible, but to manage "volatility" (the often severe "ups and downs" in "the market" (or in a market index). Although index annuity owners will not suffer any *market related* losses (because if the index declines over an interest crediting period, the annuity is credited with 0% interest), volatility in both equity indices and bond yields can and does affect what issuers of index annuities can offer to contract owners (*see "How insurers invest index annuity premiums", below*). If the insurer can manage volatility, it can offer a potentially greater share of any index growth.

Basically, a "managed volatility" account in an index annuity is invested in a multi-asset index, in which invested funds are switched back and forth among asset classes (including stocks, bonds, derivatives, and money market funds) to maintain a certain volatility "target", *instead of* managing volatility by using participation rates and caps. Many managed volatility accounts offer *no caps*. However, "no caps" doesn't mean "unlimited growth" because the whole point of the managed volatility strategy is to *not have* all one's money in a rapidly growing - highly volatile - asset (or index).

I'm willing to take more risk to get a better return

The Variable Deferred Annuity

The other kind of deferred annuity (in addition to the fixed types) is the *variable* type. The variable deferred annuity shares some characteristics with its fixed cousins:

1. It has two "phases" - the accumulation phase and the payout (or "annuity") phase
2. It contains *annuitization* options and guaranteed minimum payouts for each option
3. It is taxed identically to the fixed types, as "an annuity contract"

However, both the accumulation and payout phases of a variable deferred annuity work quite differently. At contract issue, the premium paid is allocated among the fixed and variable accounts as directed by the contract owner and used to purchase "accumulation units" in the variable accounts. At annuitization, the accumulation units are used to purchase either fixed or variable annuity units.

The deferred variable annuity has certain characteristics.

1. The contract value is expressed in terms of units that vary in value. In the accumulation phase, those are accumulation units; in the annuity phase, they're annuity units. The contract value during the accumulation phase is the sum of the value of the accumulation units (which, because they can and usually do vary in value from day to day, is why the contract is called "variable").

2. The principal (amount paid into the contract by the owner) is **not** guaranteed, except for amounts placed in the fixed account.

3. A minimum interest rate is guaranteed only with respect to the fixed account. Some variable annuity contracts do not provide for a guaranteed minimum interest rate for the fixed account.

4. Funds in the fixed account earn interest, but funds in the variable account do not; rather, any growth in those latter accounts is due to investment gains, which cause the unit values to increase. Conversely, negative investment performance will cause the value of those units to decrease. Thus, it is often incorrect to refer to "interest earned on my variable annuity".

5. A deferred variable annuity may be annuitized on either a fixed or variable basis. Annuity payout factors (described above) for fixed annuity payout options are listed in the contract, with guaranteed minimum payout amounts. In practice, the amount of any such payout option may be available at a current rate higher than (but never lower than) the guaranteed minimum. Typically, these non-guaranteed rates change as often as daily, to reflect the current interest rate environment. Once a payout option has been elected, however, the rate is guaranteed for that contract. By contrast, variable annuitization will result in purchase of annuity units that will vary in value over time, causing increases or decreases in the amount of each year's payout.

6. Contract growth (whether due to increases in the value of accumulation units or interest credited on the fixed account) is not taxable until distributed. This tax deferral is not a contractual provision, but is granted by the Internal Revenue Code.
Variable investment accounts ("subaccounts") in a deferred variable annuity

Variable investment accounts are, as was noted, similar to mutual funds, in that their growth or loss over time is the direct result of the performance of those accounts. An investment account will have a stated investment objective and will be invested in shares of stocks, bonds, real estate, or other alternative investments consistent with that investment objective. Thus, a variable deferred annuity permits the owner to be **diversified** in her investments.

Investment accounts (also called "separate accounts" or "investment sub-accounts") are similar, but not identical, to mutual funds. Reinvested dividends and capital gains are treated differently and gains in mutual funds may receive Capital Gains tax treatment while all distributions from any annuity as taxed as Ordinary Income. Shares of a mutual fund can distribute dividends paid and realized capital gains on stocks held by the fund and those distributions may be reinvested to buy more shares of the fund while those gains and dividends, when paid to a VA separate account will increase the value of the accumulation unit of that account. But there are many similarities. Investment accounts in variable annuities, for example, will be invested in specified types of securities (e.g.: large company stocks, international bonds, etc.), as is the case with mutual funds. There are no guarantees of principal or minimum return in any investment account (or in most mutual funds). Investment accounts work the same way in variable *immediate* annuities and as their performance causes the value of the annuity units to change from year to year, the amount of the annuity payment changes too.

The "fixed" account in a deferred variable annuity

The fixed account in a deferred variable annuity acts very much like a deferred fixed annuity. Principal is always guaranteed, and interest is declared and credited each year. (Some contracts offer a minimum guarantee; others do not). Monies in the fixed account are subject to the general creditors of the insurance company, while monies in the investment accounts are not (because they are held separately from the insurer's assets).

Chapter 5 - Lifetime Income Riders

There are two basic types of lifetime income riders being sold today, and one is far more popular. We'll focus on that one.

The Guaranteed Minimum Income Benefit (GMIB) rider

This is the one that is no longer popular. It's an *annuitization* option, that guarantees the owner of the deferred annuity contract to which this rider is attached (which is typically a variable deferred annuity) may elect to annuitize the "benefit base", using special annuity payout factors (which are less favorable than the factors used in normal annuitization), even if the cash value of the contract has fallen to zero. By the way, the term "guaranteed minimum income benefit rider" is an industry term. Insurers have their own "brand names" for optional riders, including this one and the GLWB rider (described below). These riders are available only on deferred annuities, both fixed and variable.

The Guaranteed Lifetime Withdrawal Benefit (GLWB) rider

This one is very, very popular. Most of the buyers of index annuities sold in recent years have chosen to purchase this optional (and extra cost) benefit. It's also very popular with buyers of variable deferred annuities. Here's how it works.

The Central Promise: A Known Percentage of the "Benefit Base"

The GLWB (we'll call it that from now on as it's less cumbersome than the full name) is a "rider", which means it "rides on top of" the annuity contract to which it is attached. It *adds* a new benefit to that contract *if* it is elected (typically, it must be added at contract inception) *and if* the contract owner "activates" it. **The benefit is an income stream that is guaranteed to last for the entire lifetime of the annuitant. This benefit *may not* be taken as a lump sum.** The *amount* of the income stream is always a *percentage of the "benefit base".*

The "Benefit Base"

The "benefit base", at contract inception, is a percentage of the cash value of the annuity contract. Usually, this percentage is 100%, although some contracts offer "initial bonus interest". This "bonus" interest may be added to the contract's cash value or only to the "benefit base". In the latter case, that interest will benefit the contract owner only if he or she activates the rider (by requesting that income payments under that rider commence) and in no other situation. (*Example: Joe contributes $100,000 to a single premium deferred annuity. The benefit base begins, thus, at $100,000 or $110,000 if the rider offers a 10% interest bonus to the benefit base.*

The benefit base may increase in two ways: (1) by application of "roll-up" interest guaranteed in the rider. Typically, this interest is payable only for a specified period (e.g.: 10 years) or until the rider is "activated" and income payments commence under the rider. (2) through a "step-up" to the benefit base. This occurs if the cash value of the contract rises to exceed the benefit base. This usually happens only with *variable* contracts where the investment performance of the separate investment accounts has been very good. If this happens during a year in which the "step-up" feature is available (in some contracts, that's every year; in others, it's only in specified years, such as every 4th year), the contract owner may elect the step-up and the benefit base will then be equal to the contract's cash value.

When the rider is activated, *partial withdrawals* that are a specified percentage of the benefit base commence. This percentage may rise with the age of the annuitant in the year of activation. (*Example: 5% for ages 50-55; 5.5% for ages 56-65; 6% for ages 66-75; and 6.5% for ages 76 and older*). The cash value of the contract will be reduced by these withdrawals. However, this income will persist for the annuitant's lifetime, **even if the contract value falls to zero.**

There are a lot of conditions imposed by this rider. For example, partial withdrawals in excess of the specified percentage will often reduce the benefit base by more than the actual withdrawal and should generally be avoided. Most contracts will not apply this to excess withdrawals that are only the Required Minimum Distributions under the contract because it's held in an IRA or qualified plan. The rider cost may be increased to a specified maximum if the owner elects a "step-up". And the rider will expire if the contract is annuitized.

The GLWB *is not an annuitization option.* Income paid under this rider is via *withdrawals*; they are not "amounts received as an annuity" and are generally fully taxable until all "gain" in the contract has been distributed. ("Gain" is the excess of the contract's cash value over the owner's "investment in the contract" - premiums paid in.

Three things to remember about the GLWB:

(1) The "benefit base" is NEVER available in a lump sum, only via these partial withdrawals.

(2) The "roll-up" interest is not a "return on your investment"! This is because it is available only as part of the withdrawals made under the rider. You can never take that money by surrendering your contract. (The surrender value of the contract **never** includes the benefit base). This can be confusing because many contracts *guarantee* a specified roll-up interest for a period of years (or until you activate the rider. That may **seem** as though you're being guaranteed that percentage as a "guaranteed interest rate". Yes, but only if you take it in the form of those withdrawals, so it's not, properly speaking, an "investment return".

(3) *You will have to live to life expectancy or longer before the money in those partial withdrawals becomes "the insurance company's money".* Until that time, you'll be receiving only money that is "yours" (because it's either a return of your premium or interest previously credited to the contract and is now part of the contract's cash value).

Now, before you get mad, let me make clear that this doesn't mean that the GLWB is a "bad deal" for the consumer. It's an *insurance* feature. It's designed to guarantee you a known minimum income for as long as you live, even if your contract doesn't perform as well as you'd hoped (which is always possible, especially with variable annuities). If you are greatly concerned over the possibility that you'll reach extreme old age and run out of income (or that your income will drop to unacceptable levels), this insurance feature may well be worth the cost (which is usually about 1% per year of the cash value of the contract).

The chart on the next page illustrates how the GLWB basically works on a variable deferred annuity. The vertical bars are the contract's benefit base ("Max Value"). The straight black diagonal line represents 6% "roll-up" interest on that benefit base. The red line represents the contract's cash value. This is obviously a *variable* deferred annuity, not any kind of fixed contract (because fixed annuities do not decline in value unless you withdraw money from them. In this case, the benefit base is "stepped up" in Year 7 and Year 9 because the cash value in that year exceeds the benefit base. The short black line from Year 7 to Year 8 represents the fact that the "roll-up guarantee will continue from that point until the expiry of the rider interest guarantee period.

A Guaranteed Lifetime Withdrawal Benefit on a Variable Deferred Annuity with a 6% "Roll-Up" Interest Rate on the Benefit Base

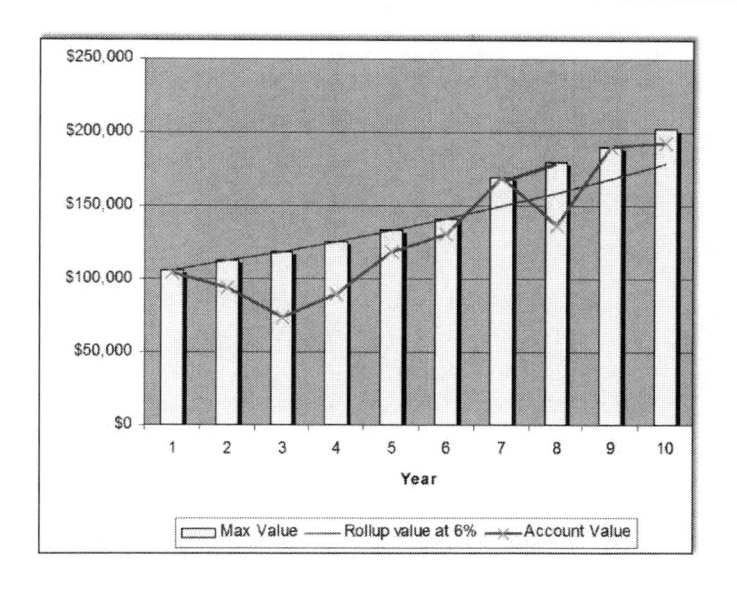

Chapter 6 - Myths About Annuities

"You can't lose money in an annuity"

This statement is flatly untrue. It is quite possible for the owner of either an immediate or deferred annuity, even one that is not *variable,* to receive less in annuity payments than he or she paid in premiums. The source of the loss in a deferred annuity could be a surrender charge, a negative Market Value Adjustment, or both. In an immediate "life only" annuity, there is no guaranteed minimum payout; even in a "life & 10 year certain" payout, the ten years of guarantee payments usually total less than the amount annuitized. What agents who make this statement usually mean is "you cannot lose money in a *fixed deferred* annuity *if you hold it for the entire surrender charge period.* But even that one is not always true. An index annuity with a 10 year surrender charge period that guarantees only 1% interest on 87.5% of premiums paid will have a *guaranteed* value of less than 97% of a single premium paid at the end of 10 years; it will take over 14 years for that value to rise to 100% of premium paid. That said, I know of *no* index annuity that has paid only *guaranteed* interest for 10 consecutive years. It is true, however, that "you can't lose money in an index annuity *due to losses in the index*" (because a period where the index declines in value results in the crediting of 0% interest for that period).

"Putting an annuity in an IRA 'wastes' the tax deferral of the annuity"

I've lost track of the number of times I've heard this one. Sadly, I hear it a lot from people who should, by their training, know better. (Sometimes, this objection is expressed as "you're paying for tax deferral you're not getting", and that's even worse). What's wrong with this statement? It betrays both a misunderstanding both of how our tax laws work and of the very idea of "suitability".

The tax deferral enjoyed by a non-qualified deferred annuity (and the above statement always refers to *deferred* annuities) owned by a human being is granted indirectly by Sections 72(b) and 72(e) of the Internal Revenue Code. That deferral treatment does not apply to annuities held in IRAs or qualified plans, so the tax deferral of an IRA annuity comes from the fact that it's IRA property and only from that. There's no "waste". Moreover, no annuity contract imposes any charge for tax-deferral, so you're not "paying for it", whether you use qualified dollars or not. But more important is the fact that the tax treatment that would apply to a deferred annuity if it were held outside an IRA is totally irrelevant to its appropriateness when it's held inside an IRA.

To see why this is the case, let's substitute some other kind of investment for "annuity" and see if the statement holds water. Let's use "small company, non-dividend paying, stock". If you invest in such a stock (or in a mutual fund investing in such stocks) and you hold your investment for more than one year, how will any profit be taxed? Any growth in the value of the stock or fund held over one year or distribution of Long Term Capital Gains will get Long Term Capital Gains (LTCG) treatment [dividends *might* or *might not* get that treatment]. Now, the tax rate for LTCG is *always* lower than the tax rate on "Ordinary Income". But if we buy that stock in our IRA, any profit will *always* be taxed at the higher Ordinary Income rate (because all taxable distributions from any IRA are always taxed at that rate). So, by the logic of that statement we're examining, we'd be "wasting" the preferential tax treatment enjoyed by "capital gains property" like stocks by putting them in our IRA. To avoid such "wasting", then, we'd **never** *fund our IRA or qualified plan with* **any** *small company stock.*

Does that make sense? Of course not, because the *suitability* of any particular type of investment doesn't depend solely on how it's going to be taxed. A deferred annuity may or may not be appropriate for Joe's IRA, depending upon a lot of factors, but the tax rate that will apply to distributions isn't one of them because all IRA property is taxed the same.

"In an Index Annuity, the Insurer Keeps the Dividends on the Index Stocks"

As we noted earlier, this is never true. The insurance company usually buys *call options* on the index value without regard to dividends. In a few cases, the option is on the index *including dividends*, in which case, the gain attributable to dividends is included in the total gain in the index and, thus, is credited to the index annuity (after application of the "moving parts").

"Annuities Have High Fees"

As we said earlier, some annuity contracts impose fees and direct charges, which may arguably be considered "high". But others impose no direct fees or charges.

"Annuities Are Bad Investments"

Right off the bat, this statement is rendered unproductive because it lumps together all annuities and judges them all by a single standard (that of "an investment"). But, as we've seen, the various types of annuities are very different from one another because they were designed to do very different jobs. Some annuity contracts may reasonably be assessed as "investments" (variable deferred annuities, certainly); others are more clearly *risk management* tools - *insurance* - (e.g.: deferred income ("longevity") annuities with no pre-Annuity Starting Date death benefit). As we've noted before, *investments* are about *acquiring profit* while *insurance* is about *avoiding loss*. This is not to say that an annuity, purchased as an investment, cannot perform badly. Clearly, that's possible. Rather, it's to say that annuities purchased chiefly to offset a loss (e.g.: having a reduced income much later in life) should be judged chiefly in their ability to do that. In other words, a *utilitarian* approach makes the most sense.

"I'm guaranteed at least a 6% return in that deferred annuity with a GLWB that has a 6% 'rollup' rate".

No, you're not! The guarantee is that the *benefit base* - the purely theoretical account from which you may take lifetime withdrawals of a given percentage (which may be less than the "rollup rate") will be credited with 6% for a given period. It's *not* a "return on investment" and if your agent claims that it is, you should be very concerned about working with that agent. The minimum guaranteed return on your investment is the interest rate guaranteed in the annuity contract itself. A variable contract guarantees no minimum interest, or even a guarantee of principal (except for money in the "fixed" account). An index annuity may guarantee less than 1%. You should not expect anything other than what the contract offers. Frankly, you're not going to be able to calculate the return until you die, because only at that point can the total payout be determined.

Annuity contracts can be simple or complicated. You should not buy *any* annuity unless and until you truly understand how it works - and how it does not work.

About The Author

John L. Olsen, CLU®, ChFC®, AEP® is an insurance agent, estate planner, author, and educator, practicing in St. Louis County, Missouri.

He holds the Chartered Life Underwriter (1983) and the Chartered Financial Consultant (1985) designations from the American College. In 2004, he received the designation of "Accredited Estate Planner" (AEP) from the National Association of Estate Planners & Councils.

John joined the financial services industry in 1973. He has worked for several insurance companies as an insurance agent, sales manager, Agency Director of Training, and Regional Marketing and Sales Consultant. In 1987, John formed Olsen Financial Group, of which he remains President. In 2015, he closed Olsen & Marrion, LLC (as Jack Marrion, his partner, retired) and opened Olsen Annuity Education, a firm specializing in fee-only consultation and training on annuity and life insurance subjects. The website is www.olsenannuityeducation.com.

John has written and taught courses in insurance; financial, retirement and estate planning; and conducted seminars for agents, planners, and lay audiences. In addition to serving his own clients, John provides case consulting services to attorneys, accountants, insurance agents, and financial advisors, and provides expert witness services in litigation involving annuities and investment products. He is a Past President of the Estate Planning Council of St. Louis, a Past President of the St. Louis chapter of the National Association of Insurance and Financial Advisors (NAIFA), and a former Director of the St. Louis chapter of the Society of Financial Services Professionals.

John has written dozens of articles on life insurance, annuities, planning software, and financial & estate planning topics, published in many industry journals and magazines and has been quoted many times in articles on annuities, life insurance, and retirement planning In 2010, John was named to the Editorial Advisory Board of *Tax Facts*, a tax reference work widely respected and used in the financial services industry. He edited the questions relating to annuities in the last several editions.

John is co-author, with Michael E. Kitces, of *The Advisor's Guide to Annuities* (5th. ed., National Underwriter Co., 2017), with Jack Marrion, of *Index Annuities: A Suitable Approach* (Olsen & Marrion, LLC, 2011), and is the author of *Taxation and Suitability of Annuities for the Professional Advisor* (2014) and *John Olsen's Guide to Annuities for the Consumer* (2015). All are available at www.olsenannuityeducation.com.

John's article, *"Annuities and Suitability: Reflections on the State of the Debate"*, appearing in the Nov, 2006 issue of the *Journal of Financial Service Professionals*, won the First Place prize in the 2006 Kenneth Black, Jr. Journal Author Award Program. In 2011, John was awarded the Paul S. Mills Scholarship by the Foundation for Financial Service Professionals, an award established to recognize the conferee's demonstrated commitment to lifelong education, volunteerism, and ethical practice.

John is a sought-after speaker, having given presentations to chapters of the Financial Planning Association, the National Association of Insurance and Financial Advisors, and the Society of Financial Services Professionals, to several Estate Planning Councils, the Missouri Society of CPAs, the Southern California Tax & Estate Planning Forum, the American Academy of Estate Planning Attorneys, several national conventions of the Financial Planning Association, the national conventions and "Arizona Institute" of the Society of Financial Services Professionals, and the Heckerling Estate Planning Institute.

John lives in Kirkwood, Missouri with his wife, Katherine and a cat named Calpurrnia. He enjoys teaching, writing, reading, classical music, cigars, and arguing almost anything. John is an adequate pistol shot, a decent folk guitarist, and a terrible golfer. He can be reached at: 131 Hollywood Lane / Kirkwood, MO 63122 / office phone: 314-909-8818 / FAX: 314-909-7912

Made in the USA
Columbia, SC
23 October 2020